MAN – THE HUNTER ...
WOMAN – IN PURSUIT ...

Recipes for everyone,
some exotic, luxurious,
some simple, inexpensive ...

But all intended to delight and please
the palate, and the senses of those
who love, or those who would like
to love ...

Also by Barbara Cartland

Books of Love, Life and Health
THE YOUTH SECRET
THE MAGIC OF HONEY
THE MAGIC OF HONEY COOK BOOK
THE FASCINATING FORTIES
MEN ARE WONDERFUL
FOOD FOR LOVE
LOVE, LIFE AND SEX

Historical Biography
THE OUTRAGEOUS QUEEN
THE PRIVATE LIFE OF CHARLES II
THE SCANDALOUS LIFE OF KING CAROL
METTERNICH
DIANE DE POITIERS

Romances
THE MAGNIFICENT MARRIAGE
THE KARMA OF LOVE
THE MASK OF LOVE
A SWORD TO THE HEART
BEWITCHED
THE IMPETUOUS DUCHESS
SHADOW OF SIN
THE GLITTERING LIGHTS
THE DEVIL IN LOVE
THE TEARS OF LOVE
A DREAM FROM THE NIGHT
NEVER LAUGH AT LOVE
THE PROUD PRINCESS
THE SECRET OF THE GLEN
THE HEART TRIUMPHANT
HUNGRY FOR LOVE
THE DISGRACEFUL DUKE
VOTE FOR LOVE
PUNISHMENT FOR A VIXEN*
A DUEL WITH DESTINY*

and published by Corgi Books
* to be published by Corgi Books

Barbara Cartland

Recipes for Lovers

CORGI BOOKS
A DIVISION OF TRANSWORLD PUBLISHERS LTD

RECIPES FOR LOVERS
A CORGI BOOK 0 552 10510 4

First publication in Great Britain

PRINTING HISTORY
Corgi edition published 1977

Copyright © 1977 by Barbara Cartland

This book is set in 10 on 11pt. Pilgrim

Corgi Books are published by
Transworld Publishers Ltd,
Century House, 61–63 Uxbridge Road,
Ealing, London W5 5SA
Made and printed in Great Britain by
Cox & Wyman Ltd., London, Reading and Fakenham

Recipes for Lovers

OTHER BOOKS BY BARBARA CARTLAND:

Romantic Novels, over 150, the most recently published being:

The Slaves of Love	The Dream and the Glory
Passions in the Sand	The Proud Princess
An Angel in Hell	Hungry for Love
The Wild Cry of Love	The Heart Triumphant
The Blue-Eyed Witch	The Disgraceful Duke
The Incredible Honeymoon	The Taming of Lady Lorinda
A Dream from the Night	Vote for Love
Conquered by Love	The Mysterious Maid-servant
The Secret of the Glen	The Magic of Love
Never Laugh at Love	Kiss the Moonlight

Autobiographical and Biographical:
The Isthmus Years 1919–1939
The Years of Opportunity 1939–1945
I Search for Rainbows 1945–1966
We Danced All Night 1919–1929
Ronald Cartland (with a foreword by Sir Winston Churchill)
Polly, My Wonderful Mother

Historical:
Bewitching Women
The Outrageous Queen (The Story of Queen Christina of
    Sweden)
The Scandalous Life of King Carol
The Private Life of King Charles II
The Private Life of Elizabeth, Empress of Austria
Josephine, Empress of France
Diane de Poitiers
Metternich—the Passionate Diplomat

Sociology:

You in the Home	Etiquette
The Fascinating Forties	The Many Facets of Love
Marriage for Moderns	Sex and the Teenager
Be Vivid, Be Vital	The Book of Charm
Love, Life and Sex	Living Together
Vitamins for Vitality	The Youth Secret
Husbands and Wives	The Magic of Honey

Barbara Cartland's Book of Beauty and Health
Men are Wonderful

Cookery:
Barbara Cartland's Health Food Cookery Book
Food for Love   Magic of Honey Cookbook

Editor of:
The Common Problems by Ronald Cartland (with a preface
by the Rt. Hon. the Earl of Selborne, P.C.).

Drama:
Blood Money
French Dressing

Philosophy:
Touch the Stars

Radio Operetta:
The Rose and the Violet (Music by Mark Lubbock)
performed in 1942

Radio Plays:
The Caged Bird: An Episode in the Life of Elizabeth
Empress of Austria. Performed in 1957.

Verse:
Lines on Life and Love

CONTENTS

STARTERS

	Page
Asparagus Tart	64
Avocado Mousse, Marie Rose Sauce	20
Borsch	68
Braised Turbot in Champagne	28
Crab Parisienne	72
Crab Rolled in Smoked Salmon	40
Cream of Mushroom Vol-Au-Vents	110
Duck Pâté	32
Fried Whiting	52
Game Soup	94
Ham Crêpes	82
Kipper Pâté	56
Kipper Soufflé with Horseradish Sauce	102
Mackerel in Sauce	98
Onion Soup	60
Orange Soup	36
Oyster Soup	44
Pâté Eggs	106
Salmon Coulibiac	76
Salmon Mousse	86
Sole Confetti	118
Sole Veronique	90
Spinach Roll with Mushroom Sauce	122
Spinach Soufflé, Marie Rose Sauce	24
Trout in Pink Coat	114
Trout with Almonds	48
Turkey and Goose Pâté	126
Watercress Soup	16

Boeuf Stroganoff, Carrots Vichy and Lettuce Salad   65
Bresse Chicken   49
Chicken in Casserole, Sweet Corn   53
Chicken Curry with Fried Parsnips   103
Chicken with Lychees   25
Chicken with Orange and Honey Sauce, Green Peas   91
Chicken with Pineapple   17
Chicken Supremes   119
Chicken with Tarragon and Fried Croquettes   73
Coq au Vin and Broccoli, Hollandaise Sauce   111
Duck in Honey, Green Peas, Lettuce and Tomato Salad   45
Duck with Green Peppers, Green Salad   37
Duck with Orange and Honey   69
Grouse Salmi, Brussels Sprouts or Leeks in Cream Sauce   77
Kidneys with Foie Gras, Green Salad   99
Lamb En Croûte   127
Lamb Cutlets in Green Aspic   123
Lamb Cutlets in Pastry, Herbs and Wine Gravy   33
Mustard Chicken, Brussels Sprouts   61
Pheasant Normandy with Braised Celery   107
Pink Chicken   115
Special Shepherds Pie, Nut Salad   57
Steak En Crêpe, croquettes   21
Steak and Kidney Pie   95
Steak Wellington, Lettuce and Tomato Salad   87
Veal à la Créme   29
Veal with Green Pepper Sauce, Tomato Salad   83
Veal with Marsala, French Beans, Cream of Spinach   41

Baked Apples	96
Blackcurrant Ice Cream, Hot Blackcurrant Sauce	34
Champagne Sorbet	38
Cheese Kisses	104
Cheese Soufflé	108
Coffee Ice Cream with Walnuts	42
Coffee Zephyrs	66
Cold Apple Meringue	58
Cold Lemon Soufflé, Hot Orange Sauce	54
Crème de Menthe Ice Cream	124
Fresh Pineapple with Kirsch	84
Grape Ice Cream, Grape Sauce	74
Grape Tart with Cream	112
Iced Chestnut Soufflé	88
Lemon Curd Meringue	22
Lemon Shortcake	92
Lemon Water Ice, Shortbread Fingers	78
Loukmades or Love Cakes with Hymethus Honey	30
Maple Syrup Ice Cream	26
Marron Glacé Ice Cream, Marron Glacé Sauce	50
Mincemeat Meringue	128
Orange Ice Cream, Lemon Sauce	62
Smoked Salmon Pâté	70
Snow Eggs	46
Strawberry Mousse with Fresh or Frozen Strawberries	18
Strawberry Ice Cream, Hot Raspberry Sauce	116
Stuffed Apple Savoury with Cheese Sables	100
Vanilla Ice Cream, White Grape Sauce	120

INTRODUCTION

As I have said so often, Love and Health are closely linked and good health depends almost entirely on the food we eat.

No man can be a good lover; no woman warm and loving unless they are well fed and all through the ages certain foods have been known to have an aphrodisiacal effect.

The Arabs and the Indians have a wealth of literature giving recipes for the increase of physical pleasure. The Chinese consider their most powerful aphrodisiac to be Bird Nest Soup, prepared from the nest of the sea-swallows. Ginger is also extolled in China as in Arabia, Turkey, Egypt and India.

But the most reliable and most powerful stimulant from the East in my opinion is Ginseng which used to be kept for the Emperors of China and is now obtainable in all our Health Stores and gives one vitality, virility and a capacity to enjoy life. Also I am convinced that the real reason why I broke the world record last year by completing twenty-one books was due to taking Ginseng with all my other vitamins.

At some time or other every sort of meat, fish, herbs and vegetables has been extolled as an infallible cure for impotence or indifference.

The Ancient Greek writer, Diphilus believed in onions; the 7th Century Paul of Aegino told his patients to eat octopus; John Gerard, a botanist and barber-surgeon in the time of Elizabeth I speaks of the carrot as 'serving in love matters'. In Elizabethan brothels, prunes were provided free of charge; later the German ones offered lettuce.

I believe that protein is essential to potency. Our bodies are made of 30 billion cells of protein and it has been estimated that a man to be a good lover needs 80 grams of protein a day. This is why I have in this book included a lot of protein and many fruits and vegetables which are of immense benefit to those who consume them.

I wish good luck and happiness to all lovers and the common sense to realize that while love will carry them ecstatically towards the stars it begins in the kitchen.

STELLA is fair, slight, sensitive and a little shy.
Michael is attracted to her but afraid of frightening her if he is too impetuous.
He plans a very special dinner for her.

MENU

WATERCRESS SOUP

CHICKEN WITH PINEAPPLE
GREEN PEAS

STRAWBERRY MOUSSE WITH FRESH OR
FROZEN STRAWBERRIES
CREAM

COFFEE

WINE: White Loire
Pouilly Blanc Fumé

WATERCRESS SOUP

Ingredients:

2 bunches Watercress	1 pint Milk
1 medium-sized Onion	2 Egg Yolks
1 oz. Butter	¼ pint Cream
1 oz. Flour	Salt and Pepper

Nigel Gordon:

Chop the watercress finely and then the onion. Melt the butter, add the watercress and onion, cover the pan and stew for about 5 minutes. Draw aside and mix in the flour and milk, stirring as you go. Bring to the boil and add salt and pepper. Simmer for 15 minutes then liquidise or put through a fine sieve. Return to the pan and add the egg yolks and cream which have been mixed together well. Bring slowly to the boil and serve with the surface scattered with leaves from some watercress.

CHICKEN WITH PINEAPPLE AND GREEN PEAS

Ingredients:

1–3 lb. Chicken	1 medium-sized Onion
1 oz. Butter	1 medium-size tin
1 oz. Flour.	Pineapple cubes
½ pint Chicken Stock	Salt and Pepper

Nigel Gordon:

Roast your chicken in a hot oven, 400°F, Mark 7, until done. Meanwhile make your sauce by melting the ounce of butter adding a finely chopped onion and sauté until soft. Then add the flour and chicken stock and stir until boiling. Add the pineapple cubes and juice, salt and pepper and keep stirring until hot. Slice the chicken and put on a serving platter. Pour over the sauce and serve with green peas which have been cooked in boiling salted water. Strain the peas and serve with a knob of butter.

STRAWBERRY MOUSSE WITH FRESH
OR FROZEN STRAWBERRIES AND CREAM

Ingredients:

2 lbs. Strawberries	¼ oz. Gelatine
¼ pint Water	3 Egg Whites
¼ lb. Sugar	½ pint Cream

Nigel Gordon:

Boil the strawberries with the sugar and water until the sugar has dissolved. Pour the mixture into the liquidiser and liquidise for a few minutes. Meanwhile, soften the gelatine in a little water and melt over a light heat. Add to the strawberry mixture and cool thoroughly. Whip the cream and egg whites until stiff. Combine the cream to the strawberry mixture and fold in the egg whites. Pour into a serving bowl and chill for a few hours in the refrigerator. Decorate with strawberries and a little fresh cream and serve with fresh or frozen strawberries which have had icing sugar sprinkled over them and soaked in kirsch.

Barbara Cartland:

The ancients believed that those who ate cress grew firm and decided in character. The Greeks recommended it for stupid people because they thought it enlivened the intellect. One of the proverbs was: 'Eat cress and learn more wit.'

Lord Bacon called it 'friendly to life'. The strawberry is beneficial to health and its delicate scent has been extolled by many famous writers.

If Michael treats Stella with tenderness and appeals to her imagination, he will win her heart and soul.

DOREEN is jolly, full of fun and very reliable and has a good appetite. Andrew likes her, but there has never been anything but friendship between them.

He wants to get married and his mother thinks that Doreen would make him an ideal wife. He is however afraid she may be unresponsive.

He orders dinner to be eaten by candlelight.

MENU

AVOCADO MOUSSE
MARIE ROSE SAUCE

STEAK EN CRÊPE
CROQUETTES

LEMON CURD MERINGUE

COFFEE

WINE: Red Burgundy
(SUGGESTION: Beaune)

AVOCADO MOUSSE, MARIE ROSE SAUCE

Ingredients:

1 Avocado Pear
½ a Chicken Stock Cube
Juice of 1 Lemon
¼ teasp. Chives
¼ teasp. Tarragon

⅛ teasp. Tabasco Sauce
1 teasp. Chopped Onion
¼ oz. Gelatine
¼ pint Cream
Salt and Pepper

Nigel Gordon:

Dice the avocado and put in the liquidiser along with the lemon juice, herbs and onion, tabasco sauce and chicken stock cube which has been dissolved in ¼ pint water, and blend until smooth. Dissolve the gelatine in 1½ tablespoons water over a gentle heat. Scrape the avocado mixture into a bowl and beat in the dissolved gelatine. Whip the cream lightly and fold into the avocado mixture and season. Put into a greased mould and into the refrigerator to set. Turn out onto a plate and decorate with tomato wedges and cucumber. Also you can add a few black olives to the decoration if you wish. Serve with a Marie Rose Sauce which is made with equal amounts of cream and mayonnaise to which you add a little worcester sauce and tomato ketchup to make it look pink in colour.

STEAK EN CRÊPE, CROQUETTES

Ingredients:

½ pint Pancake Batter
2 Fillet Steaks (thinly cut)
½ teasp. Chives
½ teasp. Parsley
½ teasp. Chervil

A pinch of Nutmeg.
½ teasp. Black Pepper
½ lb. Butter
1 tbsp. Red Wine Vinegar
¼ pint Cream

Nigel Gordon:

Make the pancake batter in the usual way and add to it the chives, parsley, chervil and nutmeg. Leave the batter to stand for an hour. Beat the steaks with a steak hammer until fairly thin and roll them in crushed black peppercorns. Fry the steaks in a tablespoon of butter for each steak. Set aside on a platter to keep hot. Pour off all the fat from the pan and pour on the vinegar and let it evaporate completely. Pour on the cream, bring to the boil and adjust the seasoning. Add the rest of the butter, but be careful not to let the sauce boil any longer. Make your pancakes and place the steak on each one. They will have to be fairly large pancakes so that you can wrap them around the steak. Pour the sauce over the steaks at the last minute and serve with croquette potatoes. Peel, boil and mash your potatoes and bind with an egg. Roll in breadcrumbs and fry in a little oil until golden brown.

LEMON CURD MERINGUE

Ingredients:

¼ lb. Puff Pastry	2 Eggs
¼ lb. Caster Sugar	3 Egg Whites
⅛ lb. Butter	6 ozs. Icing Sugar
Grated rind and juice of 1 lemon	

Nigel Gordon:

Roll out pastry and line a flan ring. Bake in a hot oven, 400°F, Mark 7, for 15 minutes. Meanwhile make the lemon curd by melting the butter and sugar over a double boiler, add the lemon juice and grated rind and stir until well mixed. Beat the eggs and add to the mixture. Keep on stirring until the mixture thickens. Remove the pastry from the flan case and pour in the lemon curd. Meanwhile beat the egg whites until firm and add the icing sugar. Keep whisking until very firm and then spoon over the lemon curd making peaks as you spoon. Put into a slow oven, 300°F, Mark 1, for 20 to 30 minutes.

Barbara Cartland:

Avocados not only contain about every vitamin and mineral we require but they are very romantic. So are, I think, the steaks boiled in paper-thin parcels with a sauce which might have been made from dreams.

Lemon Curd Meringue pleases the eye and the imagination, and if Doreen does not respond after this dinner Andrew would be a fool to marry her.

SKYE is young and inexperienced, but she has an attraction for Mark who is smart and sophisticated which he can't explain to himself.

She has consented for the first time to dine in his expensive, luxurious flat.

He chooses a dinner which he is sure will delight her.

MENU

SPINACH SOUFFLÉ
MARIE ROSE SAUCE

CHICKEN WITH LYCHEES
GREEN PEAS

MAPLE SYRUP ICE CREAM

COFFEE

WINE: Champagne
Pol Roger

SPINACH SOUFFLÉ WITH
MARIE ROSE SAUCE

Ingredients:

½ lb. Spinach
1 oz. Butter
1 oz. Flour
½ pint Milk

4 Egg Yolks
5 Egg Whites
Salt and Pepper

Nigel Gordon:

Cook the spinach in salted water, then drain well. Melt the butter and add the flour and milk. Bring to the boil and remove. When a little cool add the spinach, then beat in the egg yolks one at a time. Add plenty of salt and pepper. Whisk the egg whites until firm and fold into the spinach mixture with a metal spoon.

Turn into a prepared soufflé dish and bake in a moderate oven, 300° F, Mark 4, for 25 minutes. Serve with a Marie Rose Sauce which is equal amounts of cream and mayonnaise to which is added a little worcester sauce and tomato ketchup. Serve the soufflé immediately otherwise it will go down rapidly when it comes out of the oven.

CHICKEN WITH LYCHEES AND GREEN PEAS

Ingredients:

1–3 lb. Chicken	½ pint Chicken Stock
1 tin Lychees	1 medium-sized Onion
1 oz. Butter	(chopped finely)
1 oz. Flour	Salt and Pepper

Nigel Gordon:

Roast the chicken in a hot oven 400°F, Mark 7, until done. Meanwhile make the sauce by melting the butter, and soften the onion. Add flour and chicken stock. Bring to the boil, then add the lychees and juice. Season with salt and pepper. Slice the chicken and put onto a serving platter. Pour the lychee sauce over the chicken and serve with green peas, which have been boiled in salted water, then strained and serve with a knob of butter.

MAPLE SYRUP ICE CREAM

Ingredients:
    ½ pint Cream   2 Egg Yolks
    2 ozs. Sugar   ⅛ pint Maple Syrup
    ⅛ pint Water

Nigel Gordon:

Dissolve the sugar in the water and leave to cool. Beat the egg yolks and add the sugar syrup and continue beating until white. Then add the cream and maple syrup. Beat slowly until well mixed and put into a serving dish. Freeze for 1 hour, then whisk again to remove the icicles which form on the ice cream. Return to the freezer and freeze until hard. Serve with maple syrup and cream.

Barbara Cartland:

Spinach came originally from Persia to Spain and from them to us. The Marie Rose sauce has a very romantic appearance and glamour.

I know of no fruit which has a more subtle and glamorous taste than Lychees. Their fragility makes them appealing to a feminine woman. I could almost say the same of the succulent maple syrup which always makes me think of love.

Mark must be as gentle, tender and imaginative as the dinner.

DESMOND has for some months been in love with Isobel, who is older than himself and is married to a business tycoon who is always abroad.

Daringly he asks her to dinner at a small French restaurant near his lodgings.

When she consents he spends hours choosing the meal.

MENU

BRAISED TURBOT IN CHAMPAGNE

VEAL À LA CRÉME
FRENCH BEANS

LOUKMADES OR LOVE CAKES
HYMETHUS HONEY
CREAM

COFFEE

WINE: Red Burgundy
    (Suggestion: Fleurie)

BRAISED TURBOT IN CHAMPAGNE

Ingredients:

4 Turbot Fillets	¼ pint Cream
¼ lb. Butter	1 tbsp. Arrowroot
2 Shallots	6 tbsp. Fish Stock
¼ lb. Button Mushrooms	Salt and Pepper
½ pint Champagne	

Nigel Gordon:

First of all, boil the fish trimmings with onion, carrot, seasoning and wine, which is about 1 hour. While the stock is boiling melt half the butter and add shallots and sauté until soft. Then add the mushrooms which have been sliced, and cook for a further 5 minutes. Remove the onions and mushrooms and keep hot. Melt the remaining butter and place turbot fillets in the pan. Fry until slightly coloured. Add the onions and mushrooms, then your fish stock and ¼ pint of champagne. Season with salt and pepper and simmer for a few minutes longer. Remove the fillets and keep hot on a serving dish in a hot place. Add the cream and mix the arrowroot with a little water, add to the sauce and cook, stirring over a low heat until the sauce is smooth. Pour in the remaining ¼ pint of champagne and mix with the sauce until hot. Pour over the turbot fillets and serve immediately.

VEAL À LA CRÉME WITH
FRENCH BEANS

Ingredients:

2 Escalopes of Veal	4 Tomatoes
4 tbsp. Butter	3 tbsp. White Wine
2 Shallots (chopped)	2 tbsp. Cream
2 Cloves Garlic (chopped)	1 tbsp. Sugar
2 Green Peppers (chopped)	Salt and Pepper

Nigel Gordon:

Chop and sauté the onion and garlic in one tablespoon of the butter until clear, then chop and add the green peppers. Cook for a few minutes longer. Season with salt and pepper and add sugar. Simmer for 15 minutes. Sauté the veal in the remaining butter until cooked through. Remove the escalopes and keep warm in a warm place. Pour wine into the remaining juices and reduce by half. Add the onion, pepper and tomato mixture and then the cream, and simmer gently until hot. You can add more cream if you wish to do so. Pour over the veal and serve with french beans which have been cooked in boiling, salted water, then strained and served with a knob of butter.

LOUKMADES OR LOVE CAKES WITH
HYMETHUS HONEY AND CREAM

Ingredients:

½ oz. Beer Yeast	2 tbsp. Hot Water
3 oz. Self-Raising Flour	1 tbsp. Crushed Almonds
1 pinch Salt	1 tbsp. Brown Sugar
3 tbsp. Honey (Hymethus	1 pinch Cinnamon
is the best for this recipe)	

Nigel Gordon:

Mix the yeast, flour and salt with enough warm water to make a thick consistency but thin enough to pour, and let it stand for 1 hour to rise. Heat up some oil in a deep pan and grasp a handful of the dough with your left hand, and with your right hand detach little dollops which you throw into the boiling oil. Next to you have a bowl of honey and hot water mixed, and into that you throw the piping-hot louk-mades. Then remove them to a hot dish. Mix the almonds and brown sugar and cinnamon together and sprinkle on the loukmades. Serve with Hymethus honey, which is from Greece, and also cream.

Barbara Cartland:

Turbot has always been a Royal fish and with champagne it is Imperial. Veal assists sexual activity and Loukmades have been eaten by Greek lovers for centuries. Hymethus honey from Mt. Olympus, the home of the gods has special spiritual qualities which makes love divine.

Desmond's love-making must be as imaginative and original as the dinner he has chosen.

JEFFREY realises he has been neglecting his wife for some months and she is interested in another man. He is afraid he might lose her, and plans a special evening out, when he will try and win her back.

He chooses the dinner at an intimate little restaurant where they can talk.

MENU

DUCK PÂTÉ

LAMB CUTLETS IN PASTRY
WITH HERBS
WINE GRAVY
GREEN PEAS

BLACKCURRANT ICE CREAM
HOT BLACKCURRANT SAUCE

COFFEE

WINE: Claret
          Château du Cru Beau Caillou

LIQUEUR: Yellow Chârtreuse

DUCK PÂTÉ

Ingredients:

1 medium-sized Duck	½ lb. Lambs' Liver
1 Onion	4 tbsp. Butter
2 Bay Leaves	1 Egg beaten
4 fluid ozs. Dry	¼ lb. Fatty Bacon
White Wine	Salt and Pepper
1 teasp. Thyme	

Nigel Gordon:

Cut the duck into small pieces and marinate in the wine, to which you have added the sliced onion, bay leaves, thyme, salt and pepper. Leave it to soak for at least 1 to 2 hours. Meanwhile sauté the liver in the butter, then mince it. Add a beaten egg and season to taste with salt and pepper. Make sure that the mixture is very smooth. Line a pâté dish with half the pieces of fatty bacon and add half the liver mixture, then put a layer of the marinated duck on top and finally the other half of the liver mixture. Cover with the rest of the bacon and a bay leaf on top, and cover. Place in the oven at 350°, Mark 3, and bake for about 1 hour. Remove the cover and place a weighted plate on the pâté to compress it as it cools. Take the pâté from the casserole, remove the outside fat and place in a clean pâté dish.

LAMB CUTLETS IN PASTRY WITH HERBS, WINE GRAVY AND GREEN PEAS

Ingredients:

4 small Lamb Cutlets	½ lb. Puff Pastry
2 Lambs' Kidneys	1 pinch Thyme
2 ozs. Butter	1 pinch Tarragon
1 small Onion	1 pinch Mint
¼ lb. Mushrooms	1 pinch Rosemary

Nigel Gordon:

Cut the kidneys in half, and sauté in a little of the butter. Remove and add rest of the butter, which you melt, and sauté the onion. Add the mushrooms and all the herbs. Sauté for a few minutes longer and remove. Place the lamb cutlets in the pan and brown for a few minutes. Meanwhile roll out the pastry and place the lamb cutlets on individual pieces of the pastry. Place the onion mixture on top of each cutlet and a little of the juice from the pan. Roll up the pastry and brush with a beaten egg yolk. Put into a hot oven, 400°F, Mark 7, for 20 minutes. Serve with a herb and wine gravy. Add some wine to the rest of the pan juices with a little beef stock. To thicken, mix a little gravy powder with a little water or wine and stir into the gravy. Also serve with green peas, which have been cooked in boiling salted water. Strain the peas, and serve with a knob of butter.

BLACKCURRANT ICE CREAM WITH
HOT BLACKCURRANT SAUCE

Ingredients:

1 lb. Blackcurrants	½ pint Water
½ pint Double Cream	2 Egg Yolks
4 ozs. Sugar	

Nigel Gordon:

Wash, top and tail the blackcurrants and heat with half of the water and half of the sugar to sweeten. Strain through a fine sieve and leave to cool. Dissolve the rest of the sugar with the other half of the water. Whip the egg yolks with the sugar syrup until white and add the cream, and then half of the blackcurrant purée. Mix well. Turn into a soufflé dish, cover and place in a freezer, and freeze for 1 hour. Take out and whip again to release ice and freeze until hard. Serve with the rest of the blackcurrant purée, flavoured with either kirsch or brandy, and also heated.

Barbara Cartland:

The rule in every marriage is never tell anyone bad news until after a meal, and never bring up a controversial subject until you can settle the argument in bed.

It should be impossible to be bitter, spiteful or cruel after a dinner like this! But Jeffrey must be both conciliatory in words and positive in action.

MELISSA is a model, exotic in appearance and very elusive. She is always dieting to keep her figure.

John is wildly in love with her but he never seems to get any further.

He orders a very special, but slimming dinner at his flat.

MENU

ORANGE SOUP

DUCK WITH GREEN PEPPERS
GREEN SALAD

CHAMPAGNE SORBET

COFFEE

WINE: White Italian
           Soave Bertani

ORANGE SOUP

Ingredients:
1 tin frozen Orange Juice   1 pint Chicken Stock
1 tin Carrots   4 ozs. Single Cream

Nigel Gordon:

Liquidise the carrots with the orange juice plus two orange juice cans of water, and blend well. Add the stock and finally the single cream.

Serve well chilled and garnished with parsley.

DUCK WITH GREEN PEPPERS
AND GREEN SALAD

Ingredients:

1–4 lb. Duck
½ glass Madeira
⅓ pint Chicken Stock
1 dstsp. Flour

1½ ozs. Butter
2 dstsp. Chopped Green
   Peppers

Nigel Gordon:

Roast duck in a hot oven, 400°F, Mark 7, until done. When the duck is done remove and slice into pieces and keep hot on a serving platter. Skim the fat from the duck juice in the pan, and add the madeira and chicken stock. Reduce this by half, and thicken with the flour. Remove from the heat and add the green pepper and the butter. Stir until the butter melts into the sauce. Cover the duck with the sauce and serve with a green salad, which will consist of chopped lettuce, tomatoes, cucumber, watercress and green peppers. Toss the salad and serve with a good vinaigrette dressing.

CHAMPAGNE SORBET

Ingredients:

¾ pint of Sugar Syrup
1 quart bottle of
    Champagne
Juice of 1 Lemon

1 stiffly-beaten Egg White
2 ozs. Caster Sugar
1 dstsp. Honey

Nigel Gordon:

Mix the sugar syrup and the champagne and lemon juice in a bowl, and put into ice-cube trays and freeze in a freezing compartment of your fridge or freezer. When it is half-frozen, fold in egg white, sugar and honey, and put back into the freezer to harden. Serve in a soufflé dish, or better still, in glasses which have been cooled.

Barbara Cartland:

No-one woos a woman to-day with letters which she can treasure in her old age. Sometimes she receives flowers if she is lucky. But to be wooed with food is original and exciting.

What woman could resist the inference in this choice of menu that she is as delicate as orange blossom, delicious as a duck, sparkling as champagne, and please – not as cold as ice!

ANDORA is an actress and doing well on the television. Derek is wildly in love with her but she never seems to have time for him.

She promises, however, to have dinner with him on Sunday evening, and he chooses the dinner carefully, and has it sent in from an expensive restaurant next door.

MENU

CRAB ROLLED IN SMOKED SALMON

VEAL WITH MARSALA
CREAM SAUCE
CREAM OF SPINACH
FRENCH BEANS

COFFEE ICE CREAM WITH WALNUTS
FRESH CREAM

COFFEE

WINE: Red Burgundy
          Beaujolais Villages

LIQUEUR: Tia Maria

CRAB ROLLED IN SMOKED SALMON

Ingredients:
½ lb. White Crab	A little Cream
2 ozs. Smoked Salmon	Salt and Pepper

Nigel Gordon:

Mix the crab with the cream and seasonings. Make sure you have fairly long pieces of smoked salmon, so that you can roll up the crab in them to make them look like the shape of cigars. Decorate with wedges of tomato and thin slices of cucumber.

MENU NO. 7

VEAL WITH MARSALA CREAM SAUCE
FRENCH BEANS AND
CREAM OF SPINACH

Ingredients:

2 Escalopes of Veal	¼ pint Single Cream
2 ozs. Butter	¼ pint Marsala
1 oz. Flour	Salt and Pepper

Nigel Gordon:

Fry the escalopes in half the butter until done, put on a serving platter and keep hot. Melt the other ounce of butter, add the flour, milk and cream, and seasonings, and stir over a gentle heat until hot and smooth. Mix in the marsala and keep on stirring until hot, but not boiling. Pour over the veal escalopes and serve with french beans, which have been boiled in salted water, and serve with a knob of butter and cream of spinach. Boil the spinach in plenty of salted boiling water. Drain well and beat in some butter and a little cream, and a fair amount of black pepper. Put back on heat, stirring all the time. Turn into a serving dish and serve with the veal.

COFFEE ICE CREAM WITH WALNUTS AND FRESH CREAM

Ingredients:

½ pint Double Cream	2 Egg Yolks
2 ozs. Sugar	1 tbsp. Coffee Essence
2 fluid ozs. Water	1 tbsp. Chopped Walnuts

Nigel Gordon:

Dissolve the sugar in the water and put aside to cool. Whip the egg yolks and add the sugar syrup and whip until white and frothy. Add the coffee essence and cream, and keep on beating, then fold in the chopped walnuts. Put into a soufflé dish, cover and freeze for half-an-hour. Take out and turn over with a metal spoon, to enable the walnuts to be evenly circulated, and also this takes out the icicles which have formed. Put back into the freezer and continue to freeze until hardened. Decorate with walnuts and pipe a few cream rosettes on top before serving.

Barbara Cartland:

The sexual qualities of the first course are helped by the warmth and passion engendered by the second. The botanical name of the Walnut Tree is '*Inglans Regis*' – the Royal nut of Jupiter. Nuts influence the brain, which they resemble in shape. Best not to remember Ovid's poem:

> 'A woman, a donkey, a walnut tree
> The more you beat them the better they be.'

But Andora will want Derek to be masterful and passionate. Pleading will get him nowhere.

MAN – THE HUNTER

IDA is beautiful, cold and difficult to know, but Marcel, who is French, believes she is only deeply reserved and there is fire beneath the snow.

He takes her to a small French restaurant near his flat where they will have coffee and liqueurs after dinner. He chooses the menu very carefully.

MENU

OYSTER SOUP

DUCK IN HONEY
GREEN PEAS
LETTUCE AND TOMATO SALAD

CHEESES

SNOW EGGS

COFFEE

WINE: Red Burgundy
              Morgon

LIQUEUR: Crème de Menthe

OYSTER SOUP

Ingredients:

12 Oysters	3 tbsp. Butter
½ cup White Wine	Salt and Pepper
½ cup Cream	Cayene Pepper
¼ cup Crushed Biscuit Crackers	

Nigel Gordon:

Open the oysters and shell them. Put them in a pan and pour on their liquor which you have strained, then add the wine. Bring to the boil and then continue to simmer for a few minutes. Add the cream, crushed crackers and the butter, and season with the salt and pepper and cayenne pepper. Mix well and heat very slowly. Put into a soup tureen and serve more crushed crackers separately.

DUCK COOKED IN HONEY WITH
GREEN PEAS AND A
LETTUCE AND TOMATO SALAD

Ingredients:
   1–3 lb. Duck
   1 cup Thin Honey
   Salt
   Black Pepper

Nigel Gordon:

Prick the duck all over with a fork and rub in salt and black pepper. Put onto a wire rack and stand in a baking tin. Smear honey all over the bird. Place the duck in a medium hot oven, 375°F, Mark 5–6, and allow to cook for 40 minutes. Pour away the duck fat which has accumulated in the pan. Baste with more honey, and return to cook for another 40 minutes or until the duck is cooked. The duck's skin should be crisp and the colour of an unpeeled chestnut. Serve with a honey sauce, which is made from the honey juices, a little orange juice and water, and thickened with a little arrowroot, although this may not be necessary. Also serve with green peas, which have been boiled in salted water and strained into a serving dish with a knob of butter, and a tomato salad. Cut the tomatoes into thin slices and toss them in a good vinaigrette dressing.

CHEESES

Use various cheeses, the best being French Brie, when it is nice and ripe; Boursin, which is a herb cheese, and French Walnut Cheese.

SNOW EGGS

Ingredients:
3 Eggs (separated)
Pinch of Salt
4 ozs. Icing Sugar

½ teasp. Vanilla Essence
1 cup Milk

Nigel Gordon:

Whip the egg whites with a pinch of salt, until they stand in peaks. Fold in half the sugar and set aside. Beat the yolks slightly, and add the rest of the sugar and vanilla essence. Put into a double boiler, and add the milk slowly, stirring constantly until the mixture coats the spoon. Set the custard aside off the heat. Fill a large saucepan with boiling water, and stand over a very low heat so that the water moves very gently. With a serving spoon form the egg whites into egg shapes, and drop into the water, tapping the spoon handle to detach them. Turn them over with a skimmer, and lift out carefully and drain. Arrange on a serving dish, and pour the custard over them.

Barbara Cartland:

Oysters have been considered the first and foremost aphrodisiacal food since the Romans had them sent from Colchester to Rome for their orgies.

Honey makes those who eat it warm and loving. No woman could be frigid after such a dinner, especially with a Frenchman!

MAN – THE HUNTER

FLEUR is ambitious, but despite all her efforts to prevent it she has fallen in love with the good-looking, good-tempered, wildly-attractive Neal, who wants to marry her.

Alternatively, he will take her on any terms she offers, but she is afraid of her own heart. Neal asks her to a very special dinner feeling that her fate will be decided by the end of the evening.

MENU

TROUT WITH ALMONDS

BRESSE CHICKEN

MARRON GLACÉ ICE CREAM
MARRON GLACÉ SAUCE

COFFEE

WINE: White Muselle
Zeltinger

TROUT WITH ALMONDS

Ingredients:

2 Trout	1 tbsp. Brandy
2 ozs. Toasted Almonds	¼ pint Cream
2 ozs. Butter	Paprika Pepper
2 Spring Onions	Salt
2 ozs. Button Mushrooms	

Nigel Gordon:

Clean the trout and fry on both sides in half the butter until cooked. Take out and keep hot on a warming dish. Clean the pan and add the rest of the butter. Fry the chopped onions and mushrooms until tender. Heat the brandy, add to the pan and flame. Put out the flame with the cream, season to taste, and pour over the trout. Sprinkle the almonds on top, and serve at once.

BRESSE CHICKEN

Ingredients:

1–3 lb. Chicken	1 glass Dry White Wine
2 Chopped Shallots	2 Egg Yolks
4 ozs. Butter	½ pint Cream
1 dstsp. Flour	Salt and Pepper

Nigel Gordon:

Cut the chicken into eight pieces and season with salt and pepper. Melt the butter in a frying pan and brown the pieces lightly, then sauté the shallots until soft. Flour the pieces of chicken and return to the pan to brown a little more. Add the wine and cover with a lid and cook gently for half an hour. Mix the egg yolks and cream together, then at the last moment add this to the chicken, and stir over a good heat until the yolks cook. Dress on a dish and serve.

MARRON GLACÉ ICE CREAM WITH
MARRON GLACÉ SAUCE

Ingredients:

1 tin Chestnut Purée (unsweetened)	4 ozs. Sugar
½ pint Cream	2 fluid ozs. Water
	2 Egg Yolks

Nigel Gordon:

Make a sugar syrup by melting the sugar in the water, then allowing it to cool. Whisk the egg yolks and add the sugar syrup and continue to beat until white. Then add the cream and half the chestnut purée. Mix very well and put into a soufflé dish. Cover and freeze until hard. Mix the other half of the chestnut purée with 2 tbsp. of sugar, a little water and some brandy and serve either hot or cold.

Barbara Cartland:

Almonds in Hebrew is 'Shahad' which means awakening, and marrons have the power to make a woman feel she is loved and cosseted.

After such a seductive dinner her ambitions will seem as cold and detached from reality as a skyscraper.

MAN – THE HUNTER

HAZEL is small and wistful and every man wants to protect her. Alan does not really want to get married, but he is afraid of losing Hazel. He asks her to dinner while trying to make up his mind.

His housekeeper, who does good plain cooking, helps him with the menu.

MENU

FRIED WHITING

CHICKEN IN CASSEROLE
SWEET CORN

COLD LEMON SOUFFLÉ
HOT ORANGE SAUCE

COFFEE

WINE: White Loire
Saucerre

FRIED WHITING

Ingredients:

2 medium-sized Whitings	French Breadcrumbs
1 Egg	¼ lb. Butter

Nigel Gordon:

Wash and dry the whitings and then dip them into a well-beaten egg. After that roll in the breadcrumbs. Melt half the butter and fry the whitings until golden brown. Serve on a hot platter. Melt the other half of the butter and serve in a sauceboat.

CHICKEN IN CASSEROLE WITH
SWEET CORN

Ingredients:

1–3 lb. Chicken
1 tbsp. Butter
I tbsp. Oil
1 medium-sized Onion
 (chopped)
1 Clove Garlic
 (crushed)
¼ pint White Wine

1 tbsp. Tomato Paste
¼ pint Chicken Stock
¼ lb. Mushrooms
 (sliced)
2 medium-sized Tomatoes
 (peeled and chopped)
Salt and Pepper

Nigel Gordon:

Cut the chicken into joints, and toss in seasoned flour. Heat the butter and oil and fry the chicken joints very gently until browned all over. Drain and remove, then sauté chopped onion and garlic for about 5 minutes. Add the wine, stock, tomato paste, mushrooms, salt and pepper and bring slowly to the boil. Then return the chicken joints to the casserole and simmer for 1 hour. Drain the chicken joints and remove to a hot serving dish. Skim the fat from the casserole and add the tomatoes. Bring slowly to the boil again and taste for seasoning. Pour over the chicken and serve with sweet corn which is boiled in water for 20 to 30 minutes and served with melted butter.

COLD LEMON SOUFFLÉ WITH
HOT ORANGE SAUCE

Ingredients:

3 Eggs	½ pint Cream
2 Lemons	½ oz. Gelatine
½ lb. Caster Sugar	2 fluid ozs. Water

Nigel Gordon:

Separate the eggs and whisk the yolks, lemon rind, juice and sugar over a gentle heat until thick. Remove from the heat and keep whisking until the bowl is cold. Half whip the cream then fold into the mixture. Dissolve the gelatine in the water, then stir into the mixture. Whisk the egg white until stiff and fold into the lemon mixture. Turn into a prepared soufflé dish and put into the fridge to set. When firm remove the paper very carefully and decorate with cream and finely chopped almonds. Serve with a hot orange sauce made from the juice of two oranges heated with icing sugar, and a little wine and brandy, if you have any. You can thicken the sauce with a little arrowroot if you want to.

Barbara Cartland:

The taste of a whiting is sensitive and unearthly. The Chicken Casserole makes one think of the comfort and welcome of home.

The touch of sharp reality in the lemon mellowed by the golden glory of the orange should make Alan realise that only in marriage will he find the true perfection and fulfilment of love.

LORETTA is a reporter and it is hopeless to expect her to be on time. She is untidy, impulsive, serious-minded and big-hearted.

George, who is slow and unimaginative adores her just as she is. He has a chance to leave London to work in the country and asks Loretta to go with him. He plans the dinner knowing she'll be late.

MENU

KIPPER PÂTÉ

SPECIAL SHEPHERD'S PIE
NUT SALAD

COLD APPLE MERINGUE
CREAM

COFFEE

WINE: Claret
        Château La Tour Massac

KIPPER PÂTÉ

Ingredients:

2 filleted Kippers
4 ozs. Cream Cheese
1 tbsp. Cream

¼ teasp. Paprika
Pepper
Black Pepper
Salt

Nigel Gordon:

Poach the kippers in water for 5 minutes, and then cool slightly in the liquid. Remove and mash the flesh, then work in the cheese until it is a smooth cream. Add the paprika pepper, salt and black pepper. Then add the cream and mix well, or you can put it into the electric mixer, which is even better than doing it by hand, as it smooths it better. Adjust the seasoning and pile into a dish. Serve with either hot toast and butter, or water biscuits which have been heated, and butter.

SPECIAL SHEPHERD'S PIE WITH NUT SALAD

Ingredients:

½ lb. Potatoes
½ lb. Raw Minced Beef
1 Onion
Pinch Mixed Herbs
Salt and Pepper

1 dstsp. Worcester Sauce
1 oz. Butter
1 teasp. Bisto
1 Oxo Cube or ½
   Beef Stock Cube

Nigel Gordon:

Peel the potatoes and boil in salted water until cooked. Meanwhile cook the minced beef with the onion until nicely browned. Add the half stock cube or Oxo cube which has been dissolved in a little water, the worcester sauce, Bisto, herbs and salt and pepper. Cook for 20 minutes. Strain the potatoes, and mash with the butter and a little pepper. Put the mince in a an oven-proof dish and cover with potatoes. Place in a hot oven, 400°F, Mark 6, for 20 minutes or until the top is browned. Serve with a nut salad comprising of a cup of chopped nuts (any nuts you have – or better still a variety of them) some shredded lettuce and sliced celery. Combine the salad ingredients and serve on crisp salad leaves.

COLD APPLE MERINGUE WITH CREAM

Ingredients:

2 lbs. Cooking Apples	1 pinch Cloves
2 ozs. Sugar	2 Egg Whites
½ lb. Puff Pastry	4 ozs. Icing Sugar
1 pinch Cinnamon	

Nigel Gordon:

Roll out the pastry, line a flan dish and bake blind in the oven for 15 minutes. Remove and leave to cool. Meanwhile peel and core the apples and slice into a pan with a little water and the sugar, cinnamon and cloves, and boil until soft. Remove and leave the apples to cool. Whip the egg whites to a peak and add the icing sugar, beating all the time. Put the apple into the baked pie-crust and spoon the egg whites on top. Place in a slow oven at 300°F, Mark 2, for 30 minutes. Remove and leave to cool. Serve with cream.

Barbara Cartland:

Here are all the ordinary, commonplace ingredients of a meal transformed by loving care into a delicious and memorable menu, just as Loretta will be transformed by love and understanding into all that a man seeks and longs for in his wife.

MAN – THE HUNTER

RACHEL is spoilt, the child of rich parents and beautiful enough to have every man she meets running after her.

Perry loves her and she thinks she loves him. To-night he is determined to find out once and for all. He chooses a meal of the sort he would expect her to provide for him if they were married.

He is, as it happens, an excellent cook.

MENU

ONION SOUP

MUSTARD CHICKEN
BRUSSELS SPROUTS

ORANGE ICE CREAM
LEMON SAUCE

COFFEE

WINE: White Loire
          Sparkling Vouvray

ONION SOUP

Ingredients:

4 Onions
¼ pint Dry White wine
8 Thin Slices French Bread
Salt and Pepper

4 teasp. Flour
1½ ozs. Butter
5 ozs. Gruyère Cheese

Nigel Gordon:

Peel and slice the onions very thinly, then melt the butter in a heavy pan and add the onions. Cook until they are golden. Sprinkle with the flour and stir it in. Keep stirring while you add the white wine and 1¼ pints of boiling water, and boil for 1 minute. Meanwhile toast your bread and slice the cheese very thinly. Alternate layers of bread and cheese in a heat proof soup tureen, and pour over the hot soup. Put into the oven at 350°F, Mark 4, for 30 minutes.

MUSTARD CHICKEN WITH BRUSSELS SPROUTS

Ingredients:

1–3 lb. Chicken	1 tbsp. Butter
3 ozs. Streaky Bacon	1 Onion
¼ pint White Wine	¼ pint Chicken Stock
2 teasp. French Mustard	1 teasp. English Mustard
½ pint Double Cream	Salt and Pepper

Nigel Gordon:

Roast the chicken in a hot oven, 400°F, Mark 6, until done. Meanwhile, prepare the sauce by melting the butter in a heavy saucepan, and sauté the bacon which has been sliced, and also the sliced onion. Sauté until they are soft. Pour in the wine and stock, and bring to the boil. Blend the mustards with the cream, and stir into the sauce. Simmer gently until the sauce is the consistency of thin cream. Add salt and pepper. Remove the chicken, and slice into nice thin slices. Put onto a serving plate and pour over the sauce. Serve with small brussels sprouts, which have been boiled in salted water for 15 minutes, and serve with a knob of butter.

ORANGE ICE CREAM WITH LEMON SAUCE

Ingredients:
  ½ pint Double Cream
  2 Egg Yolks
  2 ozs. Sugar
  2 fluid ozs. Water
  ¼ pint Orange Juice

Nigel Gordon:

Melt the sugar in the water over a gentle heat. Meanwhile whisk the egg yolks until white and add the sugar syrup. Continue to whisk until frothy. Add the orange juice and then the cream. Whisk until well mixed, and put into a soufflé dish. Cover and place in the freezing compartment of your fridge and freeze for 1 hour. Remove and whisk again to remove tiny icicles that may have formed. Place back in the freezer and freeze until hard, that is about 4 to 6 hours. Serve with a hot or cold lemon sauce made from the juice and rind of 2 lemons, 1 oz. Icing Sugar, 2 fluid ozs. of water and some brandy or kirsch, if possible. Mix all the ingredients together, and stir over a gentle heat until smooth.

Barbara Cartland:

Rachel will learn by the end of the evening that Perry can offer her not only love but an adventurous, unusual life full of happiness.

No woman wants to be dull or ordinary, and in Perry she will find undiscovered depths of character she did not suspect. Perry should not be humble but strong, masterful and determined.

If he wants happiness in the future he must sweep Rachel off her feet *now*.

THE WOMAN IN PURSUIT

DAVID is reserved, controlled, and it is difficult to know what he is thinking. He is thin, often seems tired from overwork and eats in cheap restaurants, or cooks strictly for himself.

Leona has been in love with him for nearly a year, and although he takes her out he has never mentioned the word marriage.

She asks him to dinner – flowers, candlelight and a coal fire set the scene . . .

MENU

ASPARAGUS TART

BOEUF STROGANOFF
CARROTS VICHY
LETTUCE SALAD

COFFEE ZEPHYRS

COFFEE

WINE: Red Burgundy
Suggestion: Nuits St. George

ASPARAGUS TART

Ingredients:

½ lb. Puff Pastry
1 tin or 1 lb.
   Asparagus
1 tbsp. Butter
1 tbsp. Flour
2 tbsp. Milk

1 cup Double Cream
Salt and Pepper
1 pinch Grated Nutmeg
2 ozs. grated Gruyère
   Cheese

Nigel Gordon:

Make your pastry and leave to set in a cool place for an hour. Roll out, line a flan case, and bake blind for 15 minutes in a hot oven, 400°F, Mark 6. Meanwhile make a creamy sauce with the butter, flour, milk, cream, salt, pepper and nutmeg. Remove the pastry from the oven and leave to cool. Arrange the asparagus on the pastry and cover with the sauce and sprinkle with gruyère cheese. Return to the oven and cook for another 15 minutes at the same temperature until golden. Don't forget the fresh asparagus must be cooked first before using.

BOEUF STROGANOFF WITH CARROTS VICHY AND LETTUCE SALAD

Ingredients:

1 lb. Rump Steak	¼ pt Cream
1 tbsp. Chopped Onion	1 pinch Nutmeg
¼ lb. Button Mushrooms	A little Lemon Juice
2 tbsp. Butter	Salt and Pepper

Nigel Gordon:

Cut the steak in thin strips and season well with freshly ground pepper. Melt half the butter and sauté the onion until clear, then remove, add steak and brown all over. Remove the steak, add remaining butter and sauté sliced mushrooms. Return steak and onions and season well. Add nutmeg, lemon juice and cream. Do not boil, otherwise the cream will curdle. Have this dish with carrots sliced very thinly and cooked in an inch of water, with butter, sugar and salt. Cook for 10 minutes and serve with parsley, also a lettuce salad with this dish. Lettuce, cucumber and watercress dressed with a good French dressing.

COFFEE ZEPHYRS

Ingredients:

2 Egg whites	2 tasps. Instant Coffee
2 ozs. Caster Sugar	1 tablsp. chopped Walnuts

Nigel Gordon:

Whisk the egg whites until soft peaks form. Mix the coffee and sugar together and add half to the egg whites. Whisk again until stiff peaks form. Fold in the remaining sugar mixture lightly. Spoon the mixture into small heat-proof dishes and sprinkle with chopped walnuts. Bake for 15 minutes in slow oven, 300°F, Mark 1, or until slightly browned. You can serve either hot or cold.

Barbara Cartland:

Asparagus has always been a magical aphrodisiac. It was first used as a food by the Ancient Greeks and Romans about 200 B.C. It is an ingredient in many of the most famous dishes of France. A syrup of asparagus is also used by the French for rheumatic complaints.

Meat has always been a food for lovers and heroes. Since Homeric times men with an 'eye for a pretty woman' have always been large consumers of meat.

Leona must be tender and feminine during dinner and afterwards. She should appeal to his protective insincts by letting him know how much she needs him to look after *her*!

ROBERT is a senior executive, good looking, but stiff and slightly pompous.

Louise has a bet with her girl-friend that she will make him unbend. She is also, although ashamed to admit it, desperately attracted by him.

She asks him to dinner and cooks the meal.

MENU

BORSCH

DUCK WITH ORANGE AND HONEY
GREEN PEAS

SMOKED SALMON PÂTÉ

COFFEE

WINE: Claret
Suggestion: Château Liversan

BORSCH

Ingredients:

4 medium-sized cooked Beetroots	1 pint Chicken Stock
1 medium-sized Onion	1 tbsp. Parsley
2 medium-sized pieces Celery	½ tbsp. Tarragon
2 ozs. Butter	Salt and Pepper
1 tbsp. Sugar	½ pint Whipped Cream, preferably sour

Nigel Gordon:

Cut the beetroot, onion and celery into pieces and sauté in the butter and sugar until tender. Add the stock and herbs, salt and pepper and simmer for half an hour. Liquidise the soup, then reheat in a clean saucepan and serve with the whipped sour cream on the top. Put the cream on the top of the soup at the very last minute, otherwise the cream will melt.

DUCK WITH ORANGE AND HONEY

Ingredients:

1 medium-sized Duck	2 teasp. Sugar
1 cup Honey	1 tbsp. Butter
¼ cup boiling Water	1 tbsp. Flour
Juice and rind of	1 glass Chicken
1 Orange	Stock
Rind of ½ Lemon	Salt and Pepper
½ wine glass Grand	
Marnier	

Nigel Gordon:

Roast the duck in a medium oven, 350°F, Mark 3, in 3 tablespoonfuls of water for 1 hour. Remove the excess water and stock and add ½ a cup of the honey and hot water mixed. Spread over the duck and roast until done. Be careful that the duck does not burn. Meanwhile make the sauce with the butter, flour and the chicken stock and cook until boiling. Add the juice and rind of the orange and ½ lemon, the sugar, Grand Marnier and the remaining ½ cup honey. Season well, and if you think it needs more honey add more until you get it to your own liking as some people like it very sweet and others like it just a bit sour.

SMOKED SALMON PÂTÉ

Ingredients:

2 ozs. Smoked Salmon	1 teasp. Lemon
3 ozs. Curd Cheese	Juice
¼ pint Cream	Salt and Pepper
1 teasp. Chives	

Nigel Gordon:

Pound the salmon then add cheese and continue pounding until smooth. Mix in the cream, chives, lemon juice and seasoning. Serve with hot toast and butter. You can substitute the curd cheese with cream cheese, as curd cheese seems to be very hard to obtain. Also if you don't want to use toast it is equally nice with cheese biscuits.

Barbara Cartland:

The Chinese are great believers that duck stimulates a man sexually. The beetroot was so esteemed by the Ancient Greeks that they made an offering of it to their god, Apollo, on a silver dish.

Louise must flatter Robert and concentrate on him with wide-eyed admiration, make him feel important, attractive and wise.

He will certainly want to believe that he will be master in his own house.

THE WOMAN IN PURSUIT

NICHOLAS is shy and embarrassed by women. Cecilia is five years older than he is, but she is sure she will make him the right sort of wife.

She feels despairingly that only something explosive will make Nicholas respond. She chooses a dinner which is the prelude to love.

MENU

CRAB PARISIENNE

CHICKEN WITH TARRAGON
FRIED CROQUETTES

GRAPE ICE CREAM
GRAPE SAUCE

COFFEE

WINE: Chablis
Champagne Mumm Cordon Rouge

CRAB PARISIENNE

Ingredients:

½ lb. Cooked Crab
1 tbsp. Butter
1 tbsp. Flour
½ can Asparagus or
½ lb. Fresh
    Asparagus
¼ cup White Wine

½ cup Cream
Salt and Pepper
¼ cup Fresh
    Mayonnaise
1 small Egg
    (separated)

Nigel Gordon:

Melt the butter, add flour and drained liquid from the asparagus, white wine and cream. Cook over a medium heat until smooth and thickened. Season and set aside ¼ cup of the sauce. Add the crab meat and asparagus to the remaining sauce, then blend the mayonnaise and egg yolk into the ¼ cup of sauce and fold in the stiffly beaten egg white. Put the crab mixture in an oven-proof dish or crab shells, which look more attractive, spread the mayonnaise over the crab mixture and cook in a very hot oven, 450°F, Mark 7, for 15 minutes or until golden.

CHICKEN WITH TARRAGON
AND FRIED CROQUETTES

Ingredients:

1–3 lb. Chicken	1 teasp. Tarragon
Sprig of Tarragon	1 tbsp. Beurre
4 tbsp. Water	Manie
4 tbsp. Butter	Salt and Pepper
½ pint Double Cream	

Nigel Gordon:

Put the sprig of tarragon in the chicken cavity, season and put into a heavy casserole with the water and butter, cover and cook in the oven at 350°F, Mark 3, until done. Transfer the chicken to a serving platter and keep warm, then skim the fat from the liquid in the casserole, add the cream and tarragon and cook for 10 minutes. Stir in the buerre manie and cook until thickened, and season well. Slice the chicken into thin pieces and pour over the sauce. Serve this lovely and appetising dish with fried croquettes. Slice the croquettes in half, and fry in butter for 10 minutes.

MENU NO. 3

GRAPE ICE CREAM – GRAPE SAUCE

Ingredients:

½ pint Cream	⅛ pint Water
2 Egg Yolks	¼ pint Grape
2 ozs. Sugar	Juice

Nigel Gordon:

Make a sugar syrup with the water and sugar, then beat the yolks, add sugar syrup and continue beating until white and frothy. Mix the cream and grape juice which has been liquidised and strained from fresh grapes. Put into a soufflé dish and freeze for 1 hour. Mix well again to remove the ice, cover and put back to freeze for a further hour. Remove again and mix well. Put back and freeze until firm. For the sauce liquidise and strain fresh grapes, heat and add either brandy or sherry. Thicken with a little arrowroot, and serve hot with cream.

Barbara Cartland:

The *Madames* who ran the elegant *Maisons de Plaisir* in the 17th Century in France all realised the aphrodisiac importance of the *petit-souper* – the Duc de Richelieu went one step further and served grapes to his friends when every-one present – including the ladies who were often Society beauties – were completely naked.

All fish was known to have stimulating qualities es-pecially oysters and crabs. Tarragon is a valuable brain tonic.

During dinner Cecilia must make Nicholas realise how much she admires him, and not only believes in him as a man but needs him.

THE WOMAN IN PURSUIT

BASIL is ambitious, hard-headed and inclined to be ruthless. Serena knows he will want his wife to be an exceptional hostess and a good housekeeper as well as being beautiful.

She cooks the dinner but hires someone to serve it.

Lighted candles on the table, flowers in the room, Serena in floating chiffon.

MENU

SALMON COULIBIAC

GROUSE (or any game) SALMI
SMALL BRUSSELS SPROUTS
(or Leeks)
CREAM SAUCE

LEMON WATER ICE
SHORTBREAD FINGERS

COFFEE

WINE: Red Burgundy
Suggestion: Aloxe Corton

SALMON COULIBIAC

Ingredients:

½ lb. Puff Pastry	1 Onion
½ lb. Fresh Salmon	½ pint Homemade
2 Eggs (Hard boiled)	Mayonnaise
½ lb. Mushrooms	Salt and Pepper

Nigel Gordon:

Make the pastry and chill for 1 hour. Meanwhile pound the salmon which has already been cooked and mix with half the mayonnaise. Separate the egg whites from the yolks and chop finely. Sauté the onion until soft and add mushrooms and continue cooking for 5 minutes. Roll out the pastry into a rectangle and arrange the ingredients of the filling in layers, with the salmon on the bottom, the mushrooms and onion next, and finally the egg yolks and whites on top. Close up the pastry, folding over the edges from each side. Shape the coulibiac so that it resembles a fish, decorate with small round pieces of pastry-like scales and brush over with egg yolk. Bake in a hot oven, 400°F, Mark 5, for ¾ of an hour.

Add cream to the remaining mayonnaise and serve separately.

GROUSE (OR ANY GAME) SALMI
WITH SMALL BRUSSELLS SPROUTS (OR LEEKS)
IN CREAM SAUCE

Ingredients:

2 Grouse	1 tbsp. Dry Mustard
4 tbsp. Chicken Stock	1 tbsp. Butter
4 tbsp. Red Wine	1 tbsp. Flour
1 Lemon	Salt and Pepper
2 ozs. Mushrooms	Pinch Nutmeg

Nigel Gordon:

Roast Grouse, or any other game that you happen to have in the larder, in a hot oven until done. Cut into small pieces and set aside on a hot platter. Make the sauce by melting the butter, add flour and stock, red wine, juice and rind of the lemon, mustard, salt, pepper and nutmeg and stir until hot. Add mushrooms and continue to cook for a further 5 minutes. Pour over the grouse and serve with either fried croutons or small squares of puff pastry. Serve with small brussels sprouts or leeks in a well seasoned cream sauce, with salt and pepper and serve this course really hot.

LEMON WATER ICE

Ingredients:
Rind and juice of 3   1 pint Water
Lemons   2 Egg Whites
8 ozs. Caster Sugar

Nigel Gordon:

Heat the sugar in the water until dissolved, add lemon rind and boil for 10 minutes. Cool, add the lemon juice and strain the mixture into two ice-cube trays. Freeze for 1 hour, then remove and turn into a bowl and mix well with the egg whites. Replace in the cube trays and freeze until hard. Turn out into a soufflé dish and decorate with lemon rind.

SHORTBREAD FINGERS

Ingredients:
¼ lb. Butter   2 ozs. Sugar
1 lb. Flour   2 ozs. Semolina

Nigel Gordon:

Mix the butter, flour, sugar and semolina until smooth. Roll out and cut into fingers. Bake in a medium oven, 350°F, Mark 3, for 20 minutes. Serve with the lemon water ice.

Barbara Cartland:

Coulibiac is a famous Russian dish – Grouse, or any game, has always been highly valued for increasing amatory ability. Vitellius on his entry into Rome was served a feast consisting of 2,000 fish and 7,000 game birds.

Leeks contain a considerable amount of sulphur, iron, calcium and phosphorous, all of which are important to sex.

Serena must convince Basil that she believes that he can conquer the world if he wishes it.

THE WOMAN IN PURSUIT

WILLIAM is an idealist with plans to alter the world. Iona is prepared to listen to him wide-eyed, but her mother has instilled into her for years that the way to a man's heart is through his stomach! He is thin from using too much nervous energy.

She chooses a dinner which she hopes will inspire him to include her in his plans.

MENU

HAM CRÊPES

VEAL
GREEN PEPPER SAUCE
SLICED TOMATO SALAD

FRESH PINEAPPLE WITH KIRSCH

COFFEE

WINE: Red Rhône
          Côtes du Rhône

HAM CRÊPES

Ingredients:

1 Recipe Pancake
  Batter
¼ lb. Ham

½ pint Cream
3 ozs. Gruyère Cheese
1 tbsp. Butter

Nigel Gordon:

Make the pancake mixture and leave for 1 hour to set.
Meanwhile chop your ham in cubes and grate the cheese.
Make your pancakes very thinly and fill with ham. Roll up
and lay in a fireproof dish and cover with cream. Sprinkle
with the cheese and dot with butter. Bake in a hot oven,
400°F, Mark 5, for 30 minutes, or until the surface is brown.

PANCAKE BATTER

Ingredients:

4 ozs. Plain Flour
1 Egg
1 Egg Yolk
½ pint Milk

1 tbsp. Melted
  Butter
A pinch of Salt

Nigel Gordon:

Put the flour into a mixing bowl with the salt. Add the egg
yolk and a quarter of a pint of the milk. Whisk until smooth
and bubbles form on the surface, then add the melted butter
and the rest of the milk. Mix well and leave for half an hour
before using.

VEAL WITH GREEN PEPPER SAUCE, SLICED TOMATO SALAD

Ingredients:

2 Escalopes of Veal
1 Green Pepper
1 pinch Oregano
1 Artichoke
1 oz. Butter
1 oz. Flour
¼ pint Cream

Nigel Gordon:

Fry the escalopes in butter until done. Keep hot in the oven. Meanwhile make the sauce by melting the butter, add the green pepper and sauté until soft. Add the chopped artichoke and oregano. Then add your flour and cream. Keep stirring until hot but not boiling. Pour over the veal escalopes and serve with a tomato salad in which you slice your tomatoes thinly and place on a dish. Cover with honey and leave to marinate for half an hour. Surround with shredded lettuce and thin pieces of cucumber.

FRESH PINEAPPLE WITH KIRSCH

Ingredients:

1 Fresh Pineapple	1 tbsp. Cointreau
¼ Wine Glass Kirsch	¼ pint Cream
3 tbsp. Icing Sugar	

Nigel Gordon:

Slice the pineapple, cut off the outer shell and cut into segments. Toss the segments in the kirsch and cointreau, and leave to marinate, tossing the segments frequently. Whip the cream adding the icing sugar, and toss the segments in it until every piece is coated. Keep cold until time to serve.

Barbara Cartland:

Veal which has always been valued by the French was considered expensive in England in 1786 when it cost 6d per pound. The surliness of Dr. Johnson, we learn, was dispersed by the assiduous attention of Mr. Wilkes in helping him to a most succulent veal pie.

The French call tomatoes '*pommes d'amour*' or love apples. Honey has always been the food of the gods and has been considered the most effective aphrodisiac since the beginning of time.

William will want understanding and concern from his wife. Iona must show him how warmly and lovingly she will cosset him.

THE WOMAN IN PURSUIT

ROGER is the sporting 'out of doors' type with a hearty appetite. Claire knows that he hates restaurant food and longs for home cooking. He also tells her that he knows a lot about good food.

She is determined to marry him, but he is extremely elusive.

MENU

SALMON MOUSSE

STEAK WELLINGTON
LETTUCE AND TOMATO SALAD

ICED CHESTNUT SOUFFLÉ

COFFEE

WINE: Red Burgundy
Suggestion: Pommard

SALMON MOUSSE

Ingredients:

1 lb. Salmon
2 ozs. Prawns
½ pint Bechamel
    Sauce
¼ pint Mayonnaise
1 dstsp. Gelatine
3 tbsp. Water

⅛ pint Cream
1 tbsp. Anchovy
    Sauce
1 Egg White
Salt and freshly
    ground Pepper

Nigel Gordon:

Boil the salmon in a court bouillon and cool. Pound well and add cooled bechamel sauce, anchovy sauce and plenty of salt and pepper. Cream well together and add mayonnaise, and gelatine which has previously been dissolved in water, the half-whipped cream and chopped prawns. Fold in the stiffly beaten egg white and turn into an oiled No. 2 soufflé dish, and leave to set.

Turn out mousse and garnish with cucumber, water cress and fresh prawns. Serve with a lovely pink sauce which is made from equal parts of mayonnaise, tomato ketchup and cream, with a little worcester sauce added to give it an extra flavour.

BECHAMEL SAUCE

Ingredients:

½ pint Milk
½ oz. Butter

½ oz. Flour
Salt and Pepper

Nigel Gordon:

Melt the butter and add the flour, then add the milk and seasoning. Stir well until smooth and hot. If you want to add a piece of onion and some peppercorns to the milk, boil, then strain before using.

MENU NO. 6

STEAK WELLINGTON WITH
LETTUCE AND TOMATO SALAD

Ingredients:

4 lbs. Fillet of Beef	2 ozs Butter
5 Egg Yolks	1 large Onion (chopped)
1 lb. Mushrooms	Salt and Pepper
1 cup Bechamel Sauce	½ lb. Puff Pastry

Nigel Gordon:

Mince the mushrooms and onion and cook in the butter. Add the cream sauce and season well with salt and pepper. Add to the sauce the egg yolks, and continue to cook until thick.

Season the beef, roll in very hot fat until sealed. Allow to cool and coat with the purée of mushrooms. Cover with puff pastry and bake in a moderate oven, 375°F, Mark 4, for 50 minutes. Serve with a wine sauce.

WINE SAUCE

Ingredients:

1 Beef Stock Cube	¼ pint Water
Pepper (Black)	¼ pint White Wine
	Gravy Powder

Nigel Gordon:

Dissolve the stock cube in the water, and add the black pepper and three-quarters of the wine. Mix the remaining wine with the gravy powder, add to the gravy and heat, stirring all the time until fairly thick but you are able to pour.

ICED CHESTNUT SOUFFLÉ

Ingredients:

1 can Chestnut Purée	½ oz. Gelatine
2 Eggs (separated)	3 tbsp. Water
2 tbsp. Sherry	½ pint Cream
2 ozs. Sugar	Grated rind and juice of 1 Orange

Nigel Gordon:

Whisk the chestnut purée, egg yolks, sherry, sugar, orange rind and juice until mixture is thick and creamy. Dissolve the gelatine in the water and melt over a low heat, and add to the mixture. Whip the cream until thick and also fold into the mixture. Finally fold in the stiffly beaten egg whites and spoon into a soufflé dish. Leave to set and decorate with cream, almonds and orange rind.

Barbara Cartland:

The Ancient Egyptians forbade the eating of fish by priests because fish has always been accredited with the property of increasing sexual activity.

A famous poem of the 17th Century began:

'When Mighty Roast Beef was the Englishmans' Food
It ennobled our veins and enriched our Blood . . .'

Claire must convince Roger that she really loves the country and she can face hardship and discomfort if she has to. She must, however, make sure he will be her leader, not a competitor where sport is concerned.

THE WOMAN IN PURSUIT

FRANCIS is artistic, musical and very fastidious. He has taken Maureen to theatres, concerts, art collections, and telephones her nearly every day. He has however never said one word of love.

She has decided this relationship can't go on for ever and she must make a desperate effort to bring him to the point. She chooses an epicurean meal.

MENU

SOLE VERONIQUE

CHICKEN WITH ORANGE AND HONEY
GREEN PEAS

LEMON SHORTCAKE

COFFEE

WINE: White Burgundy
            Suggestion: Meursault

SOLE VERONIQUE

Ingredients:

1 Sole (filleted)	2 ozs. White Grapes
1 Shallot	1 oz. Butter
2 Mushrooms	1 tbsp. Flour
1 Bay Leaf	¼ pint Milk
1 Bouquet Garni	Lemon Juice
¼ pint White Wine	2 ozs. Cream
¼ pint Water	Salt and Pepper

Nigel Gordon:

Lay the fillets on an oven-proof dish, and cover with the shallot, mushrooms, herbs, wine, water, salt, pepper and bouquet garni, and put in a medium oven, 350°F, Mark 3, for 15 minutes. Remove the sole and keep warm. Strain the liquid from the fish and keep it to one side. Meanwhile melt the butter, add flour and fish stock, milk, lemon juice and cream. Bring it to the boil and continue to stir until the sauce thickens. Be careful not to let it curdle. Pour over the fish and decorate with seedless grapes, which have been heated through in a little lemon juice beforehand.

CHICKEN WITH ORANGE AND HONEY SAUCE AND GREEN PEAS

Ingredients:

1–3 lb. Chicken
2 tbsp. Honey
2 tbsp. undiluted
    Orange Juice

½ pint Water
2 teasp. Gravy Powder
Salt and Pepper

Nigel Gordon:

Roast the chicken in a moderate oven until done, then remove and cut into slices. Keep the chicken slices warm until needed. Meanwhile skim the surplus fat from the roasting tin, stir with a little of the water, add the rest of the water to the roasting tin and stir well. Bring the juices to the boil in a small saucepan, stir in the gravy mix, salt and pepper and cook, stirring over a low heat until smooth and thick. Pour over the chicken and serve with small green peas which have been boiled with salt and a little sugar.

LEMON SHORTCAKE

Ingredients:

5 ozs. Butter
½ lb. Plain Flour
2½ ozs. Icing Sugar
1 teasp. Vanilla Essence

¼ pint Homemade
   Lemon Curd
½ pint Cream

Nigel Gordon:

Sift the flour onto a board and add butter, icing sugar, egg yolks and vanilla essence. Knead together until a smooth paste, and leave to rest for 1 hour in a cool place. Roll out into three rounds and prick all over with a fork. Bake in a moderate oven, 350°F, Mark 3, for 15 minutes, then remove and leave to cool. Lightly whip the cream and fold in the lemon curd. Spread this evenly between the rounds of short-cake leaving the top bare. Make a white icing with icing sugar, water and a little lemon juice, making sure it is fairly thick. Spread over the top layer and decorate with thinly pared lemon rind and chopped nuts.

Barbara Cartland:

The Chinese include chicken among their long list of aphrodisiacs. Peas have always been prized for the same reason by the Arabs. The Shaykl Nefzawi in 'The Perfumed Garden', written between the years 1394 and 1433 says:

Green peas, boiled with onions and then powdered with cinnamon, ginger and cardamons create for the consumer amorous passion and strength from Cortus.

Maureen must appeal to Francis' imagination and show him that she understands his spiritual need. If she rushes him she will lose him.

IAN lives in the country, farms, and is doing well. Marianne went to London when she was eighteen but at twenty-four she longs to settle down and marry Ian.

He takes her out but she is sure he thinks of her as a 'good-time girl' who would never make a farmer happy. She asks him to dinner and chooses good country fare.

MENU

GAME SOUP

STEAK AND KIDNEY PIE

BAKED APPLES

COFFEE

WINE: Red Italian
Suggestion: Valpolicella

GAME SOUP

Ingredients:

Carcasses of Game or trimmings	2 pieces Celery
Giblets	1 Leek
1 Turnip	2 Beef stock Cubes
1 Onion	Salt and Pepper
1 Carrot	Bouquet Garni
	½ glass Dry Sherry

Nigel Gordon:

Cut the game into good sized pieces. Melt some butter, add all the vegetables and cook until tender. Add the pieces of game, stock, bouquet garni, salt and pepper and simmer for 2 hours. If the liquid reduces too much add more stock. Strain through a sieve and remove any bones if there are any. Remove grease from the top of the soup, and put into a clean saucepan. Liquidise the remaining vegetables and game, add to the soup and add the sherry. Simmer gently and, if you want, add a little cream. Serve immediately with small rounds of toast or Melba toast and butter.

STEAK AND KIDNEY PIE

Ingredients:

1 lb. Steak	¼ pint Rich Beef
½ lb. Kidneys	Stock
1 large Onion	2 tbsp. Tomato
½ lb. Mushrooms	Purée
2 Green Peppers	Seasoning
¼ pint Red Wine	½ lb. Puff Pastry

Nigel Gordon:

Cut the steak and kidneys into small cubes. Roll in seasoned flour and fry in butter for 5 minutes. Remove to a casserole and fry the onion and chopped green pepper until soft, add the mushrooms and continue to fry for a further 5 minutes. Remove to the casserole, add wine and stock, tomato purée and seasoning. Put into a medium oven, 350°F, Mark 3, for 1½ hours or until well cooked. Meanwhile roll out the pastry and leave it to rest. Remove the steak and kidney to a pie-dish and leave to cool. Place the pastry over the pie-dish, decorate and put back into the oven for a further half an hour or until golden brown.

BAKED APPLES

Ingredients:
2 large Cooking
  Apples
2 dstsp. Sultanas

½ cup Honey
½ cup Fresh Orange
  Juice

Nigel Gordon:

Core the apples and fill with the sultanas. Place in an oven-proof dish. Pour over the honey and orange juice and bake in a moderate oven, 350°F, Mark 3, until the apples are cooked through. If you wish you can add a touch of Grand Marnier or Brandy to the orange and honey, to give it extra flavour. Serve with whipped cream.

Barbara Cartland:

Until 1857 a family in England could be transported for seven years if convicted of poaching game. But Game Soup made from venison, pheasants, partridges and hare was considered an emormous stimulant to health and sex – so were kidneys.

Apple trees have the undiscovered secret of long life and in Herefordshire have been known to live for a thousand years.

Marianne must convince Ian that the one thing she longs for is a family and that she would never want to live in London if she had a child.

THE WOMAN IN PURSUIT

OLIVER is a painter and seldom has time to eat, wash or be polite. He asked Romola to model for him, and is trying to persuade her to live with him. She is twenty-five and wants to be married.

She asks Oliver to dinner to talk about the future and as he is always late has to have dishes she can 'finish off' quickly when he does arrive.

MENU

MACKEREL IN SAUCE

KIDNEYS WITH FOIE GRAS
GREEN SALAD

STUFFED APPLE SAVOURY
CHEESE SABLES

COFFEE

WINE: Sparkling Portuguese
        Suggestion: Mateus Rosé

MACKEREL IN SAUCE
(MACKEREL SGOMBRO ALLA MALTESE)

Ingredients:

4 lbs Mackerel	1 oz. Salt
4 pints Water	½ oz. Pepper
I teacup Vinegar	1 teasp. Mixed
1 sliced Onion	Herbs
3 Bay Leaves	1 sliced Lemon
12 Black	1 sliced Carrot
Peppercorns	

Nigel Gordon:

Cook the mackerel with all the ingredients for 15 minutes. When cooked cool under cold water. Fillet the mackerel and lay flat in a dish.

SAUCE FOR MACKEREL

Ingredients:

Juice of 6 Lemons	12 Spring Onions cut
2 ozs. whole Capers	into small pieces
4 ozs. diced stuffed	4 Cloves of Garlic cut
Olives	very fine
1½ pints Olive Oil	Salt and Pepper to taste
1 sliced Green Pepper	

Nigel Gordon:

Mix all the ingredients well in a glass bowl. Pour over the mackerel and leave overnight. Sprinkle with chopped parsley.

* Menu No. 9: Mackerel Sgombro Alla Maltese comes from Joseph Grech of The Battleaxes Inn, Elstree, Hertfordshire. (Manager: Fulvio Balatak).

KIDNEYS WITH FOIE GRAS
GREEN SALAD

Ingredients:
- 6 Lambs' Kidneys
- 2 tbsp. Butter
- 2 teasp. French Mustard
- 3 tbsp. Cream

- 1 small tin Pâté Foie Gras
- 3 tbsp. Port
- 1 tbsp Lemon Juice
- Brandy
- Salt and Pepper

Nigel Gordon:

Skin and sauté the kidneys in half the butter. Remove them and dice. Heat the rest of the butter, add diced kidneys, French mustard, salt, pepper and port. Heat until boiling, add brandy and flame. Mash the pâté and add to the kidneys with the cream and lemon juice. Mix well but do not boil. Cook until kidneys are tender and serve with fried croutons. Serve this dish with a lovely green salad, made up of lettuce, cucumber, watercress very finely chopped, green pepper and endive. Toss this salad with a French dressing.

STUFFED APPLE SAVOURY WITH CHEESE SABLES

Ingredients:

2 medium Eating Apples	1 teasp. Caster Sugar
1 stick Celery	Salt and Black Pepper
1 tbsp. Cream	A touch of Garlic
1 teasp. Lemon Juice	

Nigel Gordon:

Cut the tops off the apples and scoop out the flesh. Mix in a bowl with the lemon juice, diced celery, cream, salt, pepper and garlic. Coat the apple well with the cream filling. Spoon the mixture into the apple cases, and decorate with half a walnut. Serve with cheese sables, which are made from 1 oz. grated cheese, 1 oz. flour, 1½ ozs. butter, salt and pepper. Mix the cheese, flour, butter, salt and pepper until it is a dough, then roll out and cut into triangles. Brush with beaten egg and bake in a very moderate oven 375°F. Mark 4, for 10 minutes.

Barbara Cartland:

In some parts of Scotland women believe a mackerel has special stimulative powers on a man. Kidneys were great favourites with the Romans who were always worrying about their capacity to take part competently in orgies. Lettuce improves the eyesight and helps all the sensuous organs. For other ingredients in the salad, follow the poet who wrote:

'Take endive: like love it is better
Take beet for like love it is red
Crisp leaf of the lettuce shall glitter
With cress from the rivulets bed.'

Romola must appeal to Oliver's chivalrous and idealistic side – all painters have one.

NORMAN is tight-lipped and always worrying over money, although he can afford to live comfortably. He is attracted to Jane, but has not suggested marriage because she is sure he thinks her extravagant.

She plans to entertain him with a delicious dinner but on such a small expenditure that it will surprise him.

MENU

KIPPER SOUFFLÉ
HORSERADISH SAUCE

CHICKEN CURRY
FRIED PARSNIPS

CHEESE KISSES

COFFEE

WINE: Moselle
  Suggestion: Berncasteler Reisling

KIPPER SOUFFLÉ WITH
HORSERADISH SAUCE

Ingredients:

1 oz. Butter	5 Egg Whites
1 oz. Flour	4 ozs. Kipper
¼ pint Milk	Salt and Cayenne
4 Egg Yolks	Pepper

Nigel Gordon:

Melt the butter in a double saucepan, add flour and milk and stir until boiling. Cool slightly and beat in egg yolks one at a time, adding salt and cayenne pepper to taste, then work in the kipper, which has already been cooked and flaked. Whip the whites to a firm snow and carefully fold into the kipper mixture. Turn the mixture into a prepared soufflé dish and cook at 400°F, Mark 6, for 20 to 25 minutes. Remove the paper from the soufflé dish and serve immediately, with a good hot horseradish sauce.

CHICKEN CURRY WITH FRIED PARSNIPS

Ingredients:

Chicken leftovers
1 oz. Butter
1 tbsp. Curry Powder
1 tbsp. Flour
1 medium Onion

½ pint Stock
1 dstsp. Red
    Currant Jelly
¼ pint Cream
Salt and Pepper

Nigel Gordon:

Dice the chicken that you have left over and put to one side. Melt the butter, add the finely chopped onion and sauté until soft. Add the curry powder, flour, stock, red currant jelly, salt and pepper, and cook until hot. Continue to simmer for 10 minutes and add the cream and diced chicken. Cook for a further 10 minutes or until chicken is hot. Serve with fried parsnips.

Peel and slice the parsnips, boil in boiling, salted water for 5 minutes and then you can either fry on top of the cooker in a little fat, or put into a roasting tin in the oven until tender.

CHEESE KISSES

Ingredients:

¼ lb. Puff Pastry	¾ oz. Flour
Oil	½ lb. Cheddar Cheese
½ pint Milk	Salt and Pepper

Nigel Gordon:

Roll out the puff pastry very thinly and cut out stars with a tiny star cutter. Heat the oil in a deep frying pan and drop the stars a few at a time in it. Cook until puffy and golden. Drain, set aside and keep hot. Meanwhile, make the sauce with the milk, flour, cheese, salt and pepper. When the sauce is ready flame it with a little brandy if you want to give it an extra flavour. Spoon a little of the cheese sauce onto a plate. Add a few stars and top with parmesan cheese.

Barbara Cartland:

Curries of all kinds are stimulating. The Romans served cold, raw or cooked parsnips with a sauce of mead or honey, and this dish was considered by them to be powerfully aphrodisiac.

Janet must not only prove to Norman that she is not extravagant as a housekeeper, but also that her ideas are more spiritual than material.

VICTOR is conceited, and with reason, as he is on the way to becoming a tycoon. Bettina has been going out with him for over a year and he discusses his ambitions with her, but she has very little money and she suspects that he does not think she is grand enough to be his wife.

She asks him to dinner at her sister's luxurious flat and plans a candlelight dinner which will impress him.

MENU

PÂTÉ EGGS

PHEASANT NORMANDY
BRAISED CELERY

CHEESE SOUFFLÉ
COFFEE

WINE: Claret
        Suggestion: Château Corbin

PÂTÉ EGGS

Ingredients:

1 oz. Butter	1 Chicken Stock Cube
1 oz. Flour	6 Eggs
½ pint Milk	1 tin Pâté
½ pint Cream	Salt and Pepper
1 oz. Curry Powder	Parmesan Cheese

Nigel Gordon:

Hard boil the eggs, halve them and remove the yolks. Place the whites in an oven-proof dish and fill the cavities with the pâté. Make the sauce with the butter, flour, milk and cream. Add the stock cube, curry powder, salt and pepper and bring to the boil. Pour over the egg whites and sprinkle with the egg yolks and parmesan cheese. Heat in the oven at 350°F, Mark 3, until the top is browned.

PHEASANT NORMANDY WITH BRAISED CELERY

Ingredients:

1–3 lb. Pheasant	¼ glass Brandy or
2 Eating Apples	½ glass Calvados
1 oz. Butter	¼ pint Double Cream
1 Onion	Bouquet Garni
¼ pint Chicken Stock	Salt and Pepper

Nigel Gordon:

Brown the pheasant all over in the butter, add the onion and cook until golden. Flame with the brandy or calvados and when the flames subside tip on the stock. Add the apples which have been peeled, cored and sliced and the seasonings, and bouquet garni. Cover and put into the oven until cooked through. Remove the pheasant from the sauce, slice and put in a hot place to keep warm. Put the sauce in the liquidiser and liquidise, then strain into a clean plan. Add the cream and heat through. Spoon over the pheasant and serve with braised celery. Blanch the celery for a few minutes in salted water, drain and place in an oven-proof dish surrounded by brown stock, seasoning and bouquet garni. Cover and braise in the oven for about an hour or until tender. Dish the celery and strain over the gravy.

CHEESE SOUFFLÉ

Ingredients:

1 oz. Butter	4 Egg Yolks
1 oz. Flour	6 Egg Whites
¼ pint Milk	Salt and Cayenne
2 oz. Parmesan Cheese	Pepper
2 oz. Gruyère Cheese	

Nigel Gordon:

Melt the butter in a double saucepan, add flour and milk and stir until boiling. Cool for a minute, add egg yolks and cheese, salt and cayenne pepper. Whip whites until firm and carefully fold into the soufflé mixture. Turn into a prepared soufflé dish and bake in a hot oven, 400°F, Mark 5, for 25 minutes. Remove the paper and serve immediately while the soufflé is still nice and high.

Barbara Cartland:

Eggs, because of their shape, have been considered symbols of fertility all through history. Eggs, onions and honey appear frequently in the aphrodisiac dishes, (especially Arabic) of the Orient. In the Greek erotic writings, Ovid says:

> 'Eat the white shallots sent from Megara
> Or garden herbs that aphrodisiac are
> Or eggs, or honey a Hymethus flowing
> Or nuts upon the sharp-leaved pine-trees growing.'

Bettina will win Victor by flattering and making herself indispensable to him. Nothing should be too much trouble if pleases him.

DORINDA and Peregrine have been divorced for over a year and both are unhappy. Dorinda longs to be married to him again, but she is determined that he shall suggest it first.

She asks him to her rather dull little suburban house, and sends the children away for the night. He hates household chores so she prepares dinner, but has a woman in to dish it up and to clean up afterwards.

MENU

CREAM OF MUSHROOM VOL-AU-VENTS

COQ AU VIN
BROCCOLI WITH HOLLANDAISE SAUCE

GRAPE TART WITH CREAM

COFFEE

WINE: Claret
Suggestion: Clos de Cheval Blanc

CREAM OF MUSHROOM VOL-AU-VENTS

Ingredients:

½ lb. Puff Pastry	¼ pint Milk
½ lb. Mushrooms	2 ozs. Cream
1 oz. Butter	Salt, Pepper and
1 oz. Flour	Nutmeg

Nigel Gordon:

Roll out the pastry and cut into vol-au-vents. Put into a hot oven, 400°F, Mark 5, for 15 minutes. Meanwhile, make the sauce by melting the butter, add flour, milk, cream, salt, pepper and nutmeg. Stir until boiling and add the mushrooms which have been previously sliced and sautéd. Remove the top of the vol-au-vents and spoon the mushroom mixture into the cavities. Replace the tops and serve any remaining sauce with the vol-au-vents.

COQ AU VIN AND BROCCOLI
WITH HOLLANDAISE SAUCE

Ingredients:
- 1–3 lb. Chicken
- ¼ lb. Unsmoked Bacon
- 1 oz. Butter
- 2 small Onions
- ¼ lb. Button mushrooms
- 1 Clove Garlic
- ¼ pint Red Wine
- ¼ pint Chicken Stock
- Bouquet Garni
- Brandy
- Salt and Pepper

Nigel Gordon:

Roast the chicken for 1 hour, remove and cut into pieces. Heat the butter in a casserole and sauté the onions and diced bacon until brown. Add the mushrooms and continue to cook for a few minutes. Add the wine and stock, bouquet garni, garlic, salt and pepper, and heat until boiling. Place the chicken into the casserole and continue to simmer until tender. Remove the chicken, then skim the excess fat off the sauce. Put on a high heat, pour in cognac and ignite. Add a lump of sugar and reduce sauce to half its original quantity. Thicken with a buerre manie made from: 1 tbsp. flour and 1 tbsp. butter. Replace the chicken pieces and keep hot in a slow oven until ready to serve. Serve with broccoli and a good hollandaise sauce.

GRAPE TART WITH CREAM

Ingredients:
    ½ lb. Shortcrust
        Pastry
    ½ lb. White Grapes
    ½ lb. Black Grapes
    ¼ pint Apricot
        Glaze

Nigel Gordon:

Roll out the pastry, line a flan ring and bake blind in a pre-heated oven, 350°F, Mark 3, for 20 minutes. Peel and pip the grapes, and arrange in sections round the pastry. Spoon the apricot glaze over the grapes and leave to set. Decorate with a small bunch of grapes dipped in egg white and caster sugar and place in the middle of the tart.

Barbara Cartland:

Mushrooms have always been invested with a Special Magic. To the French the use and understanding of mushrooms is part of their magnificent culinary art. They contain ergosterol in large quantities – this is the raw material as it were of Vitamin D – they also contain a large proportion of sulphur and calcium and are the nearest approach to meat in the vegetable kingdom.

There is no pride in love. Dorinda must tell Peregrine that she cannot live without him and all she wants is his love.

A PINK DINNER is a lovely way of celebrating the first time you met or the first time you made love. Have pink candles on the table and pink flowers, pink table-napkins, and of course wear a pink dress.

MENU

TROUT IN PINK COAT

PINK CHICKEN

STRAWBERRY ICE CREAM
HOT RASPBERRY SAUCE

COFFEE

WINE: Lanson Pink Champagne
             or
          Vin Rosé

LIQUEUR: Rosé

TROUT IN PINK COAT

Ingredients:

2 Trout	4 tbsp. Fresh
¼ lb. Fresh Cod	Breadcrumbs
or Haddock	1 tbsp. White Wine
Juice of ¼ Lemon	1 Egg Yolk
½ oz. Butter)	1 tbsp. Cream
(unsalted)	Salt and Pepper
½ lb. Smoked Salmon	

Nigel Gordon:

Clean the trout and remove insides including the back bone, if possible. Meanwhile mince the cod or haddock, add the breadcrumbs, egg yolk, white wine, lemon juice, butter, cream, salt and pepper. Mix well together and fill the insides of the trout with the mixture. Tie the trout round with string, and then either fry in butter until done, or put into a fireproof dish in the oven, with a little wine until cooked. Remove the string when the fish is cooked, leave to cool, and wrap the smoked salmon round the trout completely covering them.

PINK CHICKEN

Ingredients:

1–3 lb. Chicken
¼ pint Chicken Stock
1 teasp. English
    Mustard (ready mixed)

½ pint Cream
2 tbsp. Worcester
    Sauce
2 tbsp. Tomato Purée

Nigel Gordon:

Boil or roast the chicken until tender. Slice in pieces, place on a dish and keep warm. Meanwhile, make the sauce with the cream, stock, mustard, worcester sauce and tomato purée. Bring it just short of the boil and pour over your chicken, mixing well, and sprinkle with paprika pepper and parsley.

STRAWBERRY ICE CREAM WITH HOT RASPBERRY SAUCE

Ingredients:

1 lb. Strawberries	½ pint Cream
2 ozs. Sugar	¼ pint Water
2 Egg Yolks	

Nigel Gordon:

Wash the strawberries and place in the liquidiser, and liquidise. Boil the sugar in the water until sugar dissolves. Beat the egg yolks until white and add the sugar syrup, add the cream and then the strawberry purée and mix well. Turn into a soufflé dish; cover and freeze for 1 hour. Take out, mix well again, to remove the icicles, cover and freeze again until hard. This ice cream is served with a raspberry sauce, which is raspberry purée heated with kirsch or brandy, sugar and a very small amount of arrowroot mixed with a little water. Stir until hot and serve immediately.

SPECIAL OCCASIONS

A WHITE DINNER is for Wedding Anniversaries, and it is so important to celebrate each year of marriage by being alone with the person you love and married on that particular day.

Send the children to Grandma. Put on your wedding gown (if you can get into it) and buy your husband a buttonhole.

A candlelit dining-room, and remember to make love to each other with words as well as actions.

Only one hot dish to save the 'bride' from having to leave the table.

MENU

SOLE WITH CONFETTIE

CHICKEN SUPREMES

VANILLA ICE CREAM
WHITE GRAPE SAUCE

COFFEE

CHAMPAGNE: Moet et Chandon (It is worth it even if you save up all the year)

LIQUEUR: Cointreau

SOLE CONFETTI
(Recipe from Claridges Hotel London.)

Ingredients:

1 Sole	2 Mushrooms
1 Tomato (chopped)	(chopped)
1 teasp. Tarragon	1 Sherry Glass
3 tbsp. Cream	White wine
Chopped Parsley	Salt and Pepper
1 Shallot (chopped)	

Nigel Gordon:

Skin and fillet the sole and fold in half. Then place in a fireproof dish with the onion, tomato which should be skinned and de-seeded before you chop it, mushrooms, tarragon, white wine, salt and pepper. Cover with buttered, greaseproof paper, and cook for 10 minutes in a moderate oven, 350°F, Mark 4. Remove fillets and place on a heated serving dish and keep hot. Meanwhile, reduce the stock a little and add the cream. Heat through and spoon over the fish. Sprinkle with chopped parsley. The sauce will look like confetti, with the different vegetables through it.

CHICKEN SUPREMES
COLD AND DECORATED WITH
WHITE FLOWERS

Ingredients:

2 Chicken Breasts
1 Egg (beaten)
½ oz. Butter
¼ pint well flavoured
    White Sauce
1 squeeze Lemon
    Juice

1 tbsp. Cream
1 tbsp. Flour
1 oz. Fresh
    Breadcrumbs
½ tbsp. Oil
1 Egg Yolk
Salt and Pepper

Nigel Gordon:

Trim the supremes and coat with seasoned flour, dip in the beaten egg and then in breadcrumbs. Fry in the butter and oil, turning them once, and cook for about 20 minutes altogether. Remove them from the pan, drain on kitchen paper and cool. Mix the sauce, lemon juice, egg yolk and cream, and re-heat without boiling, re-season if necessary, and pour over the chicken. Leave to get cold and decorate the dish with white flowers.

VANILLA ICE CREAM, WHITE GRAPE SAUCE

Ingredients:

4 Egg Yolks	4 ozs. Sugar
¼ pint Water	1 pint Cream
1 teasp. Vanilla	1 lb. White Grapes
Essence	1 teasp. Arrowroot
1 tbsp. Kirsch	
or Brandy	

Nigel Gordon:

Dissolve the sugar in the water. Meanwhile, whip the egg yolks until white, and add the sugar syrup, keep on whipping until frothy then add the cream and vanilla essence. Put in a soufflé dish, cover with foil, and place in a freezing compartment for 1 hour. Remove after the hour, and whip again to remove the icicles. Cover again and freeze until firm. Make a sauce by liquidising the grapes and straining them into a pan. Keep a little back to mix with the arrowroot, and heat until boiling. Add the arrowroot and kirsch or brandy, and serve hot with the ice cream.

SPECIAL OCCASIONS

A GREEN DINNER can celebrate a birthday, an achievement, a win on the Pools or the Stock Exchange, or to impress your friends. Have green candles and table napkins.

MENU

SPINACH ROLL
MUSHROOM SAUCE

LAMB CUTLETS IN GREEN ASPIC
GREEN VEGETABLES
GREEN SALAD

CRÈME DE MENTHE ICE CREAM

COFFEE

WINE: Portuguese Vinho Verde
            Casal Garcia

LIQUEUR: Green Chartreuse

SPINACH ROLL WITH MUSHROOM SAUCE

Ingredients:

1 lb. Spinach
4 Eggs (separated)
6 ozs. Mushrooms
1 oz. Butter
½ oz. Flour
¼ pint Milk

¼ pint Cream
Grated Nutmeg
Grated Parmesan
    Cheese
Salt and Pepper

Nigel Gordon:

Cook the spinach and drain well. Stir in half an ounce of the butter, the egg yolks, salt and pepper. Whip the egg whites until firm and fold into the spinach mixture. Spread on a Swiss Roll tin lined with greaseproof paper, which has been greased with butter or margarine and dust well with the parmesan cheese. Bake in a hot oven, 400°F, Mark 7, for 15 minutes. Slice the mushrooms finely and sauté in the rest of the butter. Add the flour, seasonings and nutmeg, then the milk and cream and heat slowly until hot, but not boiling. Turn out the spinach roll, spread with some of the mushroom mixture and roll up. Serve with the rest of the mushroom sauce.

LAMB CUTLETS IN GREEN ASPIC

Ingredients:

4 Lamb Cutlets	1 pint Water
Green Colouring	1 oz. Powdered Aspic

Nigel Gordon:

Grill the lamb cutlets until done, then leave to cool in a deep dish. Meanwhile, make the aspic jelly by dissolving the aspic in the pint of boiling water, then colour it green until it is the shade of green that you require. Leave the aspic until it is half set, then pour over the cutlets. Leave it to set, then surround the cutlets with more of the aspic jelly which you chop up, and decorate round the cutlets to look as if they are in the sea. Serve with a bowl of green peas, and a bowl of green beans, and a side salad of lettuce, cucumber and watercress chopped up finely.

CRÈME DE MENTHE ICE CREAM

Ingredients:

6 Egg Yolks
6 dstsp. Sugar
1 pint Double Cream
½ lb. Dark
    Chocolate

1 miniature bottle of
    Crème de Menthe
¼ pint Single Cream
Peppermint

Nigel Gordon:

Beat the egg yolks with the sugar until creamy. Beat in double cream and crème de menthe. Chop half the chocolate into little pieces, and fold into the mixture. Freeze for 6 hours, stirring once or twice during this time to even out the chocolate chips.

Make the sauce by melting the rest of the chocolate in a double boiler very slowly, and add the single cream, previously heated, and a few drops of peppermint. Serve hot in a sauceboat. You can add crème de menthe to the sauce instead of the peppermint, if you wish.

SPECIAL OCCASIONS

Many people like to celebrate for the New Year.

Here is a special dish to see the Old Year out and the New Year in.

MENU

TURKEY AND GOOSE PÂTÉ

LAMB EN CROÛTE
CARROTS
GREEN SALAD

MINCEMEAT MERINGUE
CREAM

COFFEE

APERITIF: Rum Punch

CHAMPAGNE: (If you can afford it)
Louis Roederer

MENU NO. 4

TURKEY AND GOOSE PÂTÉ

Ingredients:

4 ozs. Cold Turkey	4 ozs. Pickled
4 ozs. Cold Goose	Walnuts
4 ozs. Ham	1 Chicken Stock Cube
1 oz. Gelatine	½ pint Boiling
2 ozs. Breadcrumbs	Water
	Salt and Pepper

Nigel Gordon:

Mince the turkey and goose meat finely, and put into a bowl, then add the breadcrumbs. Mince the ham twice and add to the turkey and goose mixture. Chop the walnuts finely and add to the turkey mixture. Then dissolve the chicken stock cube and gelatine in the boiling water, stirring until smooth. Allow time to cool, then add to the turkey mixture beating well until all the ingredients are evenly blended. Check the seasoning, adding salt and pepper to taste. Put the mixture into 1½ pint pudding basin and press down well. Cover with a piece of foil and leave in a cool place for at least 3 hours, or until set. Remove the foil, and place upside down on a serving platter. Lift up slowly so that the pâté comes out evenly and doesn't break, and decorate with cucumber and tomato wedges. Serve the pâté with hot toast and butter.

LAMB EN CROÛTE

Ingredients:

2 lb. Leg of Lamb (boned)	A little Sherry
2 Lambs' Kidneys	2 ozs. Butter
½ lb. Puff Pastry	¼ lb. Mushrooms
1 pinch Tarragon	1 pinch Thyme
	1 pinch Rosemary

Nigel Gordon:

Dice and toss the kidneys in a little of the butter in a frying pan. Stir a little sherry into the pan, and add the mushrooms and herbs. Pour this mixture into the hole in the leg, left by the removal of the bone. Re-form the leg of lamb by sewing the end up with a trimming needle. Rub the leg with the remaining butter and place in a hot oven, 400°F, Mark 7, for 15 minutes to seal the meat. Remove from the oven and allow to cool, then wrap in the finely rolled-out pastry. Brush the top with egg yolks, and replace in the oven for another 30 minutes, or until the pastry is brown. Serve with a wine gravy, from the juices from the lamb; also carrots and a green salad.

MINCEMEAT MERINGUE

Ingredients:
    ½ lb. Puff Pastry
    1 lb. Homemade
        Mincemeat

    2 Egg Whites
    4 ozs. Icing Sugar

Nigel Gordon:

Roll out the pastry very thinly and line a flan ring. Bake blind in a hot oven, 400°F, Mark 7, for 15 minutes, and remove from the oven. Fill with the mincemeat mixture and leave to cool. Whip the egg whites until firm, and add the sugar. Whip for a few minutes more and pipe or spoon onto the mincemeat. Place in a cool oven, 250° to 300°F, Mark 2, for 30 minutes, or until the meringue is just turning brown.